Christmas DEVOTIONAL

Celebrating Who Jesus Is and Why He Came

CHRIS BAXTER

Christmas Devotional: Celebrating Who Jesus Is and Why He Came
Copyright © 2018 Chris Baxter.

All rights reserved. No portion of this book may be reproduced, stored in a retrieval system, or transmitted in any form or by any means – electronic, mechanical, photo-copy, recording, scanning, or other – except for brief quotations in critical reviews or articles, or as specifically allowed by the U. S. Copyright Act of 1976, as amended, without prior written permission of the publisher.

Published by MC Publishing.
www.respitefortheweary.com

Scripture quotations taken from the New American Standard Bible®, Copyright © 1960, 1962, 1963, 1968, 1971, 1972, 1973, 1975, 1977, 1995 by The Lockman Foundation. Used by permission. (www.Lockman.org) The words highlighted in bold in the selected scriptures are for writer's emphasis.

ISBN: 978-0-578-40922-1
Graphic Design: Hannah Thomas

Printed by IngramSpark Print-On-Demand Services.

To
All Those Who
Want to Celebrate
Who Jesus Is
and
Why He Came

To the Reader

Dear Reader,

In the rush of the holidays, we often miss "the why" of Christmas. The hustle and bustle of gift-buying, party-hopping, and tree-trimming can quickly diminish the purpose of celebrating the birth of our Lord and Savior, Jesus Christ. This 25-day devotional is meant to give you a designated time to slow down and reflect over the holy-days. Choose to read these specific scriptures about our King as a personal quiet time, or as a family devotional. Take time to be still, meditate, and savor His goodness; and then... celebrate the wonderful truths of who Jesus is, and what He gives each heart that believes.

O Come let us behold Him,

Chris Baxter
www.respitefortheweary.com

Table of Contents

JESUS IS...

Day 1 - The Savior 1
Day 2 - The Prince of Peace 3
Day 3 - The Son of God, One with God 5
Day 4 - The Lamb of God 7
Day 5 - The Good Shepherd 9
Day 6 - The Light of the World 11
Day 7 - The Bread of Life 13
Day 8 - The Living Water 15
Day 9 - The Great Servant 17
Day 10 - The Master Teacher 19
Day 11 - The Friend 21
Day 12 - The Redeemer 23

HE CAME TO GIVE...

Day 13 - Eternal Life 27
Day 14 - His Holy Spirit 29
Day 15 - Freedom 31
Day 16 - Forgiveness 33
Day 17 - Love 35
Day 18 - Joy 37
Day 19 - Peace 39
Day 20 - Comfort 41
Day 21 - Contentment 43
Day 22 - Wisdom 45
Day 23 - Discipline 47
Day 24 - Hope 49
Day 25 - Celebrate Who Jesus Is and Why He Came 51

Who is This Jesus?

Savior

DAY 1
Jesus is the Savior

Isaiah 45:21b-22
And there is no other God besides Me, a righteous God and a **Savior**; there is none except Me. Turn to Me and be saved, all the ends of the earth; for I am God, and there is no other.

Matthew 1:21
And she (Mary) will bear a Son, and you shall call His name Jesus... for it is He who will **save** His people from their sins.

1 John 4:14-15
And we beheld and bear witness that the Father has sent the Son to be the **Savior** of the world. Whoever confesses Jesus is the Son of God, God abides in him and he in God.

1 Timothy 1:15
It is a trustworthy statement, deserving full acceptance, that Christ Jesus came into the world to **save** sinners, among whom I am foremost of all.

Titus 3:4-5
But when the kindness of God our **Savior** and His love for mankind appeared, He saved us, not on the basis of deeds which we have done in righteousness, but according to His mercy, by the washing of regeneration and renewing by the Holy Spirit.

My Child,

I am your Savior. No one else can rescue you from the darkness and evil in this world. I am here for you; call on Me and I will come to you. I am mighty to save.

Immanuel

Prince of Peace

DAY 2
Jesus is the Prince of Peace

Isaiah 9:6
...and His name will be called...the **Prince of Peace**.

Ephesians 2:17-18
And He came and preached **peace** to you who were far away, and **peace** to those who were near; for through Him we both have our access in one Spirit to the Father.

Colossians 1:19-20
For it was the Father's good pleasure for all the fullness to dwell in Him, and through Him reconcile all things to Himself, having made **peace** through the blood of His cross.

Psalm 119:165
Those who love Your law have great **peace**, and nothing causes them to stumble.

Mark 4:38-39
And He Himself was in the stern, asleep on the cushion; and they awoke Him and said to Him, "Teacher, do you not care that we are perishing? And being aroused, He rebuked the wind and said to the sea, "Hush, **be still**." And the wind died down and it became perfectly calm.

My Child,

I am your Prince of Peace. Realize I have the power and authority to calm every storm that arises in your heart and mind. Cry out to Me and I will answer. The wind and the waves might continue in your circumstances, but My incomprehensible peace will be ever present in your soul.

Immanuel

Son of God

DAY 3
Jesus is the Son of God, One with God

Ephesians 4:4-6
There is **one body** and **one Spirit**, just as you were called in one hope of your calling; one Lord, one faith, one baptism, one God and Father of all who is over all and through all and in all.

Philippians 2:2-5
Have this attitude in yourselves which was also in Christ Jesus, who although He existed in the **form of God**, did not regard equality with God a thing to be grasped, but emptied Himself, taking the form of a bond-servant, and being made in the likeness of men. And being found in appearance as a man, He humbled Himself by becoming obedient to the point of death, even death on a cross. Therefore God also highly exalted Him, and bestowed on Him the name which is above every name, that at the name of Jesus every knee should bow, of those who are in heaven, and on earth, and under the earth, and that every tongue should confess that Jesus Christ is Lord, to the glory of God the Father.

John 10:30
Jesus said, "I and the Father are **one**."

I Timothy 2:5-6a
For there is **one** God, and **one** mediator also between God and man, the man Jesus Christ who gave Himself as a ransom for all...

Hebrews 1:3
His **Son**...is the radiance of God's glory and the exact representation of His nature, and upholds all things by the word of His power.

My Child,
I am the Son of God. All the majesty and power that exists in God My Father also dwells in Me. I came to earth to be the bearer of His invisible image (Colossians 1:15). Look to Me. My character, as I walked My life out on earth, and you will see God. Learn from Me, and you will find peace.

Immanuel

Lamb of God

DAY 4
Jesus is the Lamb of God

Genesis 22:8
And Abraham said, "God will provide for Himself the **lamb**..."

Exodus 12:21-23
Then Moses called for all the elders of Israel, and said to them, "Go and take for yourselves **lambs** according to your families, and slay the Passover **lamb**... and apply some of the blood that is in the basin to the lintel and the two doorposts... and when the Lord sees the blood ...He will pass over the door and will not allow the destroyer to come in to your houses to smite you."

John 1:29
(John) saw Jesus coming to him, and said, "Behold, the **Lamb** of God, who takes away the sin of the world!"

1 Peter 1:18-19
Knowing that you were not redeemed with perishable things like silver or gold from your futile way of life inherited from your forefathers, but with precious blood, as of a **lamb** unblemished and spotless, the blood of Christ.

Isaiah 53:7
He was oppressed and He was afflicted, yet He did not open His mouth; like a **lamb** that is led to slaughter, and like a sheep that is silent before its shearers, so He did not open His mouth.

My Child,
I am the Lamb of God. Your sin must be dealt with before you can enter My Father's holy presence; and because I am holy, I am the only One who can settle the matter. My blood shed at the cross covered you so that you then could also become holy in God's sight. Accept My sacrifice, as your sacrifice... and live with Me forever.

Immanuel

Good Shepherd

DAY 5
Jesus is the Good Shepherd

Micah 5:2
And you, Bethlehem, land of Judah, are by no means least among the leaders of Judah; for out of you shall come forth a Ruler, who will **shepherd** My people Israel.

Isaiah 40:11
Like a **shepherd** He will tend His flock,
In His arm He will gather the lambs,
And carry them in His bosom;
He will gently lead the nursing ewes.

Psalm 23:1-3
The Lord is my **shepherd**,
I shall not want.
He makes me lie down in green pastures;
He leads me beside quiet waters,
He restores my soul;
He guides me in paths of righteousness For His name's sake.

John 10:11-14
I am the **good shepherd**; the **good shepherd** lays down His life for the sheep. He who is a hired hand, and not a shepherd, who is not the owner of the sheep, sees the wolf coming, and leaves the sheep and flees, and the wolf snatches them and scatters them. He flees because he is a hired hand and is not concerned about the sheep. I am the **good shepherd**, and I know My own and My own know Me.

My Child,
I am your Good Shepherd. I know you, and I want to carry you, quiet you, guide you, and restore your soul. Let My rod and staff comfort you as you walk out your days. I am here morning, noon, and night.

Immanuel

Light of the World

DAY 6
Jesus is the Light of the World

Numbers 6:24-26
The Lord bless you, and keep you; the Lord make His face **shine** on you, and be gracious to you; the Lord lift up His countenance on you, and give you peace.

Isaiah 60:1-2
Arise, shine; for your **light** has come, and the glory of the Lord has risen upon you. For behold, darkness will cover the earth, and deep darkness the peoples; but the Lord will rise upon you and His glory will appear upon you.

Psalm 27:1
The Lord is my **light** and my salvation; Whom shall I fear? The Lord is the defense of my life; Whom shall I dread?

Psalm 119:105
Thy Word is a lamp to my feet, And a **light** to my path.

John 1:2-4
He was in the beginning with God. All things came into being by Him, and apart from Him nothing came into being that has come into being. In Him was life, and the life was the **light** of men.

John 8:12
Jesus said, "I am the **light of the world**; he who follows Me shall not walk in darkness but shall have the **light** of life."

My Child,
I am the Light of the World. There is no darkness in Me at all. Let My word bring light to your path (Psalm 119:105). I know what your day will bring, so choose to stay by My side and obey My words. Will you allow me to "light your lamp and illumine your darkness"? (Psalm 18:28).

Immanuel

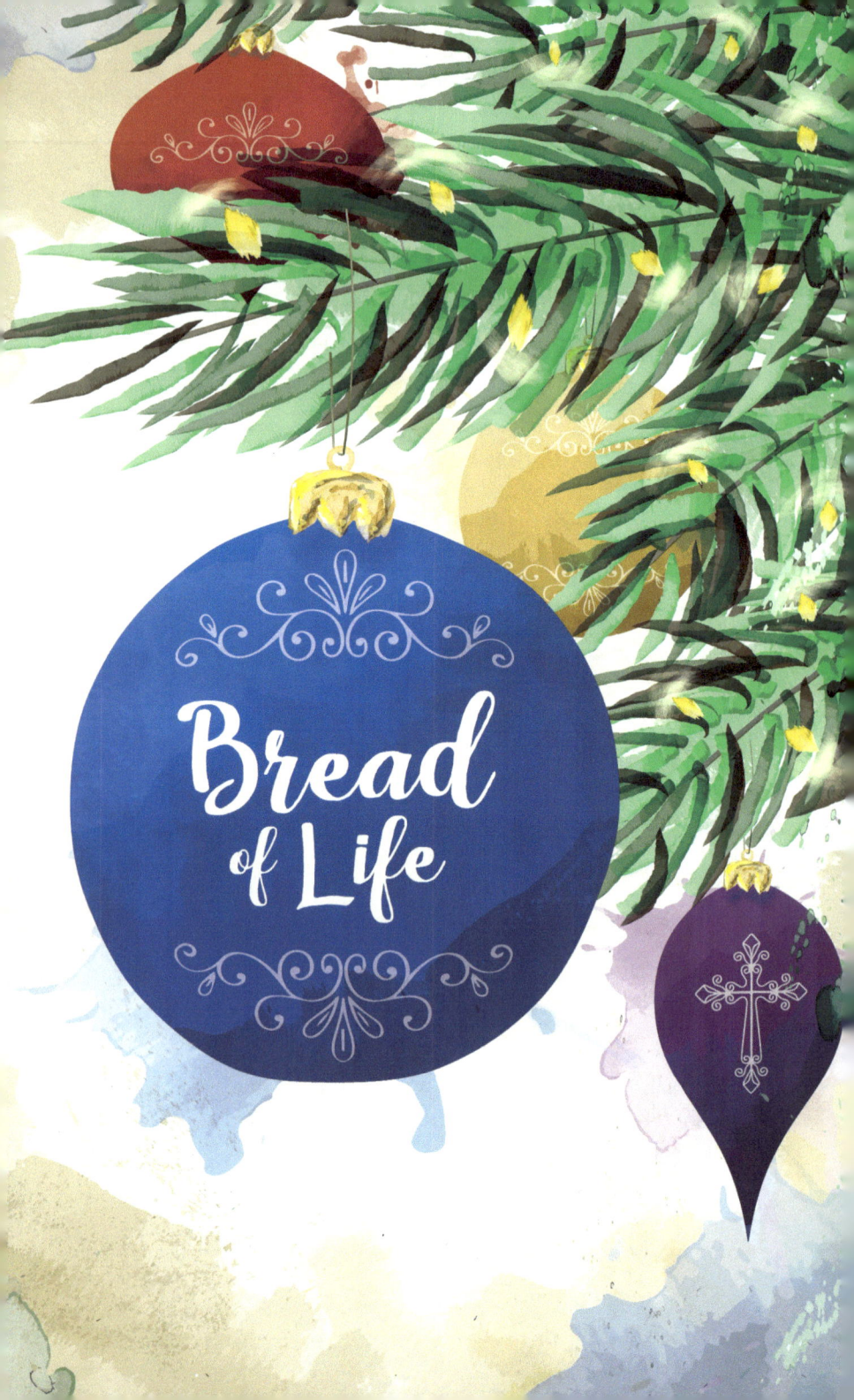

Bread
of Life

DAY 7
Jesus is the Bread of Life

Exodus 16:4, 13-15
Then the Lord said to Moses, "Behold I will rain **bread** from heaven for you."...And in the morning there was a layer of dew around the camp. When the layer of dew evaporated, behold, on the surface of the wilderness there was a fine flake-like thing, fine as the frost on the ground. When the sons of Israel saw it, they said to one another, "What is it?" For they did not know what it was. And Moses said to them, "It is the **bread** which the Lord has given you to eat."

John 6:32-33
Jesus therefore said, "... it is My Father who gives you true **bread**... which comes down out of heaven, and this **bread** gives life to the world."

John 6:35
Jesus said, "I am the **bread** of life; he who comes to Me shall not hunger, and he who believes in Me shall never thirst."

Luke 22:19
And when He had taken some **bread** and given thanks, He broke it, and gave it to them saying, "This is My body which is given for you..."

Psalm 34:8
O **taste** and see that the Lord is good; how blessed is the man who takes refuge in Him.

My Child,
I am the Bread of Life—the only One that can satisfy the deepest longings of your soul. My body was broken for you, so that you may have a never-ending portion of My mercy and My love. "Take and eat..." (Matthew 26:26).

Immanuel

Living Water

DAY 8
Jesus is the Living Water

Psalm 42:1-2
As the deer pants for the **water** brooks,
So my soul pants for You, O God,
My soul **thirsts** for God, for the living God; When shall I come and appear before God?

Isaiah 41:17-18
The afflicted and needy are seeking **water**, but there is none, and their tongue is parched with thirst; I, the Lord, will answer them Myself, as God of Israel I will not forsake them. I will open rivers on bare heights, and springs in the midst of valleys; I will make the wilderness a pool of water, and the dry land a fountain of water.

John 4:14
Jesus said, "Whoever drinks of the **water** that I shall give him shall never thirst; but the **water** that I shall give him shall become in him a well of **water** springing up to eternal life."

Revelation 22:17
And let the one who is thirsty come; let the one who wishes take the **water** of life without cost.

Ephesians 3:19
(I pray you will) know the love of Christ which surpasses knowledge, that you may be **filled up** to all the fullness of God.

Psalm 23:5
...my **cup** overflows...

My Child,
I am the Living Water. As I pour Myself into you, you will be continually cleansed and purified. I long to revive, refresh, and renew your strength by washing you with My word. Do you thirst for Me? Then go to the fountain that never runs dry.

Immanuel

Great Servant

DAY 9
Jesus is the Great Servant

Isaiah 42:1
God said (concerning Jesus), "Behold, My **Servant**, whom I uphold; My chosen one in whom My soul delights. I have put My spirit upon Him; He will bring forth justice to the nations."

Isaiah 52:13
Also... "Behold, My **Servant** will act wisely; He will be high and lifted up, and greatly exalted."

Matthew 20:28
Jesus said, "... the Son of Man did not come to be served, but **to serve**, and to give His life as a ransom for many."

John 13:5
Jesus rose from supper...and taking a towel, He girded Himself about. Then He poured water into the basin, and began to **wash** the disciples' feet.

Matthew 20:32-34
And Jesus stopped and called them, and said, "What do you want Me to do **for you**?" They said to Him, "Lord, we want our eyes to be opened." And moved with compassion, Jesus touched their eyes; and immediately, they regained their sight and followed Him.

My Child,

I am the Servant. Do you want to see the wonders of My sacrificial love in your everyday life? Ask Me to open your eyes to My acts of adoration on your behalf. I "long to be gracious to you, and I wait on high to have compassion on you" (Isaiah 30:18). Let Me bear your burdens.

Immanuel

Master Teacher

DAY 10
Jesus is the Master Teacher

Isaiah 9:6
...and His name will be called Wonderful **Counselor**...

John 1:14
And the Word became flesh and dwelt among us, and we beheld His glory, glory of the only begotten from the Father, full of grace and **truth**.

Matthew 11:28-30
Jesus said, "Come to Me, all who are weary and heavy-laden, and I will give you rest. Take My yoke upon you and **learn** from Me, for I am gentle and humble in heart; and you shall find rest for your souls. For my yoke is easy and My load is light."

John 13:13
Jesus said, "You call Me **Teacher** and Lord; and you are right, for so I am."

Psalm 25:4-5
Make me know Your ways, O Lord; **teach** me Your paths. Lead me in Your truth and **teach** me. For You are the God of my salvation; For You, I wait all the day long.

My Child,
I am the Master Teacher. Read My word and seek to know Me as "the way, the truth, and the life" (John 14:6). In so doing, you will find peace and rest in your soul. Come to Me. As your Wise Counselor, hear Me say, "This is the way, walk in it" (Isaiah 30:21).

Immanuel

Friend

DAY 11
Jesus is the Friend

Exodus 33:11
And it came about, whenever Moses went out to the tent, the pillar of cloud would descend and stand at the entrance of the tent; and the Lord would speak with Moses... face to face, just as a man speaks to his **friend**.

Proverbs 18:24b
There is a **friend** who sticks closer than a brother...

Proverbs 17:17
A **friend** loves at all times...

John 15:12-13
This is My commandment, that you love one another, just as I have loved you. Greater love has no one than this, that one lay down his life for his **friends**.

Romans 5:8
But God demonstrates His own **love** toward us, in that while we were yet sinners, Christ died for us. Much more then, having now been justified by His blood, we shall be saved from the wrath of God through Him.

My Child,

I am your Friend; and I died and rose again to seal this relationship. Do you realize that I am the only One who knows you inside out? I desire to sit with you, walk with you, talk with you, and listen to you. I can take care of your worries, your hurts, your dreams—"Cast them all on me because I care for you" (I Peter 5:7). There is not one person on this earth that can "out-friend" Me.

Immanuel

Redeemer

DAY 12
Jesus is the Redeemer

Titus 2:14
(Christ Jesus) gave Himself for us, that He might **redeem** us from every lawless deed and purify for Himself a people for His own possession, zealous for good works.

Galatians 3:13-14
Christ **redeemed** us from the curse of the law, having become a curse for us, for it is written, "Cursed is everyone who hangs on a tree." He **redeemed** us in order that in Christ Jesus the blessing of Abraham might come to the Gentiles, so that we might receive the promise of the Spirit through faith.

Job 19:25
And as for me, I know that my **Redeemer** lives...

Psalm 103:1,4
Bless the Lord, O my soul, and all that is within me, bless His holy name... who **redeems** your life from the pit; who crowns you with lovingkindness and compassion.

Isaiah 43:1
Do not fear, for I have **redeemed** you; I have called you by name; you are Mine!

My Child,
I am your Redeemer. I paid your ransom with My life so that you could be set free from sin and death. It was My life for yours. Remember the good news: I rose again from the dead in order to give you My Spirit. I am calling your name; let me redeem you. I can make beauty from ashes (Isaiah 61:3).

Immanuel

Why Did He Come?

Eternal Life

DAY 13
Jesus Came to Give Eternal Life

Isaiah 43:13
Even from **eternity** I am He, and there is none who can deliver out of My hand; I act and who can reverse it?

John 11:25-26
Jesus said, "I am the resurrection and the life; he who believes in me shall live even if he dies, and everyone who lives and believes in me shall **never die**. Do you believe this?"

John 3:16
For God so loved the world that He gave His only begotten Son, that whoever believes in Him should not perish, but have **eternal life**.

1 John 5:11-12
And the witness is this: that God has given us **eternal life**, and this life is in His Son. He who has the Son has life; he who does not have the Son of God does not have life.

Romans 6:4
Christ was raised from the dead through the glory of the Father, so we too might walk in newness of **life**.

John 10:10
Jesus said, "I came that they might have **life**, and might have it abundantly."

My Child,

I came to give you eternal life. Do you understand that when you believe in Me, you will live forever? Let Me enter in your heart now, so that we can start this abundant life together while you live out your days on this earth. With Me, you will experience a newness of life through the presence of My Spirit. Let's walk this forever-life together with joy.

Immanuel

Holy Spirit

DAY 14
Jesus Came to Give Us His Holy Spirit

John 14:15-16
Jesus said, "If you love Me, you will keep My commandments. And I will ask the Father, and He will give you another **Helper**, that He may be with you forever."

Luke 11:13
Jesus said, "If you then, being evil, know how to give good gifts to your children, how much more shall your heavenly Father give the **Holy Spirit** to those who ask?"

Romans 8:10-11
And if Christ is in you, though the body is dead because of sin, yet the spirit is alive because of righteousness. But if the **Spirit** of Him who raised Jesus from the dead dwells in you, he who raised Christ Jesus from the dead will also give life to your mortal bodies thorough His **Spirit** who indwells you.

John 16:14
Jesus said, "He (the **Holy Spirit**) will bring glory to Me by taking from what is Mine and making it known to you."

Galatians 5:22-23
The fruit of the **Spirit** is love, joy, peace, patience, kindness, goodness, faithfulness, gentleness, and self-control.

My Child,

I came to give you My Spirit. The reason I lived, died, and rose again was so that I could then dwell inside you. My Spirit will guide you, help you, and comfort you. You cannot keep my commandments on your own; it is My Spirit that will enable you to do what I ask. Let Me abide in you so that you can walk in assurance moment by moment as you listen to my words of truth.

Immanuel

Freedom

DAY 15
Jesus Came to Give Us Freedom

Luke 4:18
Jesus said, "The Spirit of the Lord is upon Me, because He has anointed Me to preach the gospel to the poor. He has sent Me to proclaim release to the captives, and recovery to the blind, to set **free** those who are downtrodden."

Galatians 5:1
It was for **freedom** that Christ set us **free**; therefore keep standing firm and do not be subject again to a yoke of slavery.

John 8:31-32
Jesus said, "If you abide in My word, then you are truly disciples of Mine; and you will know the truth, and the truth will make you **free**."

Psalm 142:7
Bring my soul **out of prison**,
So that I may give thanks to Your name;
The righteous will surround me,
For You will deal bountifully with me.

Romans 6:6-7, 11
Knowing this, that our old self was crucified with Him, that our body of sin might be done away with, that we should no longer be slaves to sin; for he who has died is **freed** from sin...Even so consider yourselves to be dead to sin, but alive to God in Jesus Christ.

My Child,
I came to give you freedom. Do not let the worries of this world entangle you. I am bigger than your problems, and I am stronger than your addictions. Give them to me, so that I can then fill your empty hands and heart with abundant, yet intangible riches: forgiveness, redemption, and the power of My Spirit.

Immanuel

Forgiveness

DAY 16
Jesus Came to Give Forgiveness

John 1:8-9
If we say we have no sin, we are deceiving ourselves, and the truth is not in us. If we confess our sins, He is faithful and righteous to **forgive** our sins and to cleanse us from all unrighteousness.

Colossians 1:13-14
For He delivered us from the domain of darkness, and transferred us to the kingdom of His beloved Son, in whom we have redemption, the **forgiveness** of sins.

Psalm 103:12
As far as the east is from the west, so far has He **removed** our transgressions from us.

Isaiah 1:18
"Come now, and let us reason together," says the Lord, "Though your sins are as scarlet, they will be **white as snow**; though they are red like crimson, they will be like wool."

Micah 7:19
He will again have compassion on us; He will tread our sins underfoot. Yes, You will **cast all our sins** into the depths of the sea.

My Child,

I came to give forgiveness. The bad news is: you and all mankind have sinned against the one and only Holy God. The good news is: I took care of your sins at the cross so that you could enter into this holiness. I took the wrath that your sins deserve so that you can stand unblemished. Your punishment was poured onto Me so that God's love could be poured into you. Never, never doubt my forgiveness—I did not die in vain.

Immanuel

Love

DAY 17
Jesus Came to Give Love

John 15:13
Greater **love** has no one than this, that one lay down his life for his friends.

Romans 5:5
...and hope does not disappoint, because the **love** of God has been poured out within our hearts through the Holy Spirit who was given to us.

Romans 5:8
But God demonstrates His own **love** toward us, in that while we were yet sinners, Christ died for us.

1 Corinthians 13:4-8
Love is patient, love is kind, and is not jealous; **love** does not brag and is not arrogant, does not act unbecomingly; it does not seek its own, is not provoked, does not take into account a wrong suffered, does not rejoice in unrighteousness, but rejoices with the truth; bears all things, believes all thing, hopes all things, endures all things. **Love** never fails.

1 John 4:16
And we have come to know and have believed the **love** which God has for us. God is **love**, and the one who abides in **love** abides in God, and God abides in him.

My Child,
I came to give you love. There is no greater love on this earth than the love that I possess for you. I took off my crown of righteousness and replaced it with a crown of thorns so that you could live with Me now and forever. I did not have to do this; I wanted to.

Immanuel

Joy

DAY 18
Jesus Came to Give Joy

Matthew 2:10-11
And when they saw the star, they rejoiced exceedingly with great **joy**. And they came into the house and saw the Child with Mary His mother; and opening their treasures they presented to Him gifts of gold and frankincense and myrrh.

John 15:9-11
Just as the Father has loved Me, I have also loved you; abide in My love. If you keep My commandments, you will abide in my love; just as I have kept My Father's commandments, and abide in His love. These things I have spoken to you, that My **joy** may be in you, and that your **joy** may be made full.

James 1:2-4
Consider it all **joy**, my brethren, when you encounter various trials, knowing that the testing of your faith produces endurance. And let endurance have its perfect result, that you may be perfect and complete, lacking in nothing.

Acts 3:6, 8
In the name of Jesus Christ...(the paralytic) stood upright and began to walk; and he entered the temple with them, walking and **leaping and praising** God.

Nehemiah 8:10b
...the **joy** of the Lord is your strength.

My Child,
I came to give you joy. You must know, there is such a vast difference between happiness and joy. Happiness is surface and temporary; joy runs deep and is eternal. Happiness depends on circumstances, and it cannot withstand any trial; however, the joy that I give you is permanent and powerful, no matter the circumstance, no matter the trial. Let My joy abound in your heart each day.

Immanuel

Peace

DAY 19
Jesus Came to Give Peace

John 14:27
Peace I leave with you; My **peace** I give to you; not as the world gives, do I give to you. Let not your heart be troubled, nor let it be afraid.

Psalm 29:11
The Lord will give strength to His people; the Lord will bless His people with **peace**.

Isaiah 26:3-4
The steadfast of mind You will keep in perfect **peace**, because he trusts in You. Trust in the Lord forever, for in God the Lord, we have an everlasting Rock.

Philippians 4:6-7
Be anxious for nothing, but in everything by prayer and supplication with thanksgiving let your requests be made known to God. And the **peace** of God, which surpasses all comprehension, shall guard your hearts and your minds in Christ Jesus.

Ephesians 2:14
For He Himself is our **peace**...

My Child,
I came to give you peace. No other meditation rituals or mind-practices can compare to the serenity I can give your soul. The more you understand who I am in My word, the more you will crave the quietness that only I can give. Hear Me say to you each day, "In repentance and rest you shall be saved, in quietness and trust is your strength" (Isaiah 30:15).

Immanuel

Comfort

DAY 20
Jesus Came to Give Comfort

John 14:18
I will not leave you as orphans; I will **come to you**.

Matthew 5:4
Jesus said, "Blessed are those who mourn, for they shall be **comforted**."

Psalm 23:4
Even though I walk through the valley of the shadow of death, I fear no evil; for You are with me. Your rod and Your staff, they **comfort** me.

Psalm 34:18-19
The Lord is **near** the brokenhearted and saves those who are crushed in spirit. Many are the afflictions of the righteous; but the Lord delivers him out of them all.

Isaiah 61:1-3
The Spirit of the Lord God is upon me, because the Lord has anointed me to bring good news to the afflicted; He has sent me to bind up the broken-hearted... to **comfort** all who mourn, to grant those who mourn in Zion, giving them a garland instead of ashes, the oil of gladness instead of mourning, the mantle of praise instead of a spirit of fainting. So they will be called oaks of righteousness, the planting of the Lord, that He may be glorified.

My Child,

I came to give you comfort. Your afflictions will not go unnoticed by Me. I too was afflicted, so I understand. Be convinced that I am present with you in your trial, and I will hold your hand each step of the way until you reach the other side. In the meantime, hear Me whisper My words of encouragement and peace; let My words of truth bind up your broken heart.

Immanuel

Contentment

DAY 21
Jesus Came to Give Contentment

Philippians 4:11-13
Not that I speak from want; for I have learned to be **content** in whatever circumstances I am in. I know how to get along with humble means, and I also know how to live in prosperity; in any and every circumstance I have learned the secret of being filled and going hungry, both of having abundance and suffering need. I can do all things through Christ who strengthens me.

Colossians 1:17-18
And He (Jesus) is before all things, and in Him all things hold together. He is also the head of the body, the church; and He is the beginning, the first born from the dead; so that He Himself might come to have **first place** in everything.

Philippians 3:7-8
But whatever things were gain to me, those things I have counted loss for the sake of Christ. More than that, I count all things to be loss in view of the surpassing value of **knowing Christ Jesus my Lord**, for whom I have suffered the loss of all things, and count them but rubbish in order that I may gain Christ.

Psalm 73:25-26
Whom have I in heaven but Thee?
And besides Thee, I desire nothing on earth.
My flesh and my heart may fail,
But God is the strength of my heart and my **portion** forever.

My Child,

I came to give you contentment. You will obtain this fulfillment if, and only if, I am the Lord of your life. When I have first place in your heart, you will not want anything else. Daily yield to Me, and I will faithfully satisfy the longings of your heart and soul.

Immanuel

Wisdom

DAY 22
Jesus Came to Give Wisdom

John 14:26
But the Helper, the Holy Spirit, whom the Father will send in My Name, He will **teach** you all things, and bring to your remembrance all that I said to you.

Psalm 143:8-10
Let me hear Your lovingkindness in the morning; for I trust in You; teach me the way in which I should walk; for to You I lift up my soul. Deliver me, O Lord, from my enemies; I take refuge in You. Teach me to do Your will, for You are my God; let Your **good Spirit lead me** on level ground.

Jeremiah 29:11-13
"For I know the plans that I have for you," declares the Lord. "Plans for welfare and not calamity, to give you a future and a hope. Then you will call upon Me and come and pray to Me; and I will listen to you. And you will **seek Me and find Me**, when you search for Me with all your heart."

Proverbs 3:13-14
How blessed is the man who finds **wisdom**, and the man who gains understanding. For its profit is better than the profit of silver, and its gain than fine gold.

Colossians 2:2-3
In Christ Himself... are hidden all the treasures of **wisdom** and knowledge.

My Child,
I came to give you wisdom, knowledge, and understanding; seek Me and you will find these jewels. My words bring life and light to your present day and your future. Trust My words, and then obey them outright — for I give wisdom generously to those who ask without doubting (James 1:5).

Immanuel

Discipline

DAY 23
Jesus Came to Give Discipline

Proverbs 3:11-12
My son, do not reject the **discipline** of the Lord, or loathe His reproof; for whom the Lord loves He reproves, even as a father, the son in whom he delights.

Hebrews 12:9-11
Furthermore, we had earthly fathers to discipline us, and we respected them; shall we not much rather be subject to the Father of our spirits, and live? For they disciplined us for a short time as seemed best to them, but He **disciplines us for our good**, that we may share in His holiness. All discipline for the moment seems not to be joyful, but sorrowful; yet to those who have been trained by it, afterwards it yields the peaceful fruit of righteousness.

Lamentations 3:31-33
For the Lord will not reject forever, for if He causes grief, then He will have **compassion** according to His abundant lovingkindness, for He does not afflict willingly, or grieve the sons of men.

My Child,

I came to give discipline—because I love you. You must know, there are two kinds of discipline that you will inevitably experience as you live out your days. One type happens as a result of disobedience. When you sin, I do grant forgiveness; however, the consequences of the sin will still follow. This, hopefully, will teach you not to walk down that path again. The other type of discipline comes as a result of circumstances that I allow into your life. They may not feel good at the time, but trust that I am at work. You are My child, and My goal is to make you more like Me—and remember, I suffered on the cross and it was glorious, because I gained... you. So just as gold is refined by fire, so your soul will be made beautiful through the various afflictions in life that cause you to depend on Me. Let Me have My way with you; trust My refining hands.

Immanuel

Hope

DAY 24
Jesus Came to Give Hope

Romans 5:3-5
And not only this, but we also exult in our tribulations, knowing that tribulation brings about perseverance; and perseverance, proven character; and proven character, **hope**; and **hope** does not disappoint, because the love of God has been poured out within our hearts through the Holy Spirit who was given to us.

Colossians 1:27
God willed to make known...this mystery...which is Christ in you, the **hope** of glory.

I Timothy 4:10
For it is for this we labor and strive, because we have fixed our **hope** on the living God, who is the Savior of all men, especially of believers.

Lamentations 3:21-25
This I recall to mind, therefore I have **hope**. The Lord's lovingkindnesses indeed never cease, for His compassions never fail. They are new every morning; great is Your faithfulness. "The Lord is my portion," says my soul, "Therefore I have **hope** in Him." The Lord is good to those who wait for Him, to the person who seeks Him.

Romans 5:13
Now may the God of **hope** fill you with all joy and peace in believing, that you may abound in **hope** by the power of the Holy Spirit.

My Child,

I came to give you hope. When I am living and reigning in you, you can face today, tomorrow, and forever. Let me walk with you today so that I can fill your heart with song. Also, remember this is not your home. Live with the great anticipation that you will someday enter heaven... a place that possesses "an eternal weight of glory far beyond all comparison" (II Corinthians 4:17). Live on earth, with the hope of heaven in your heart.

Immanuel

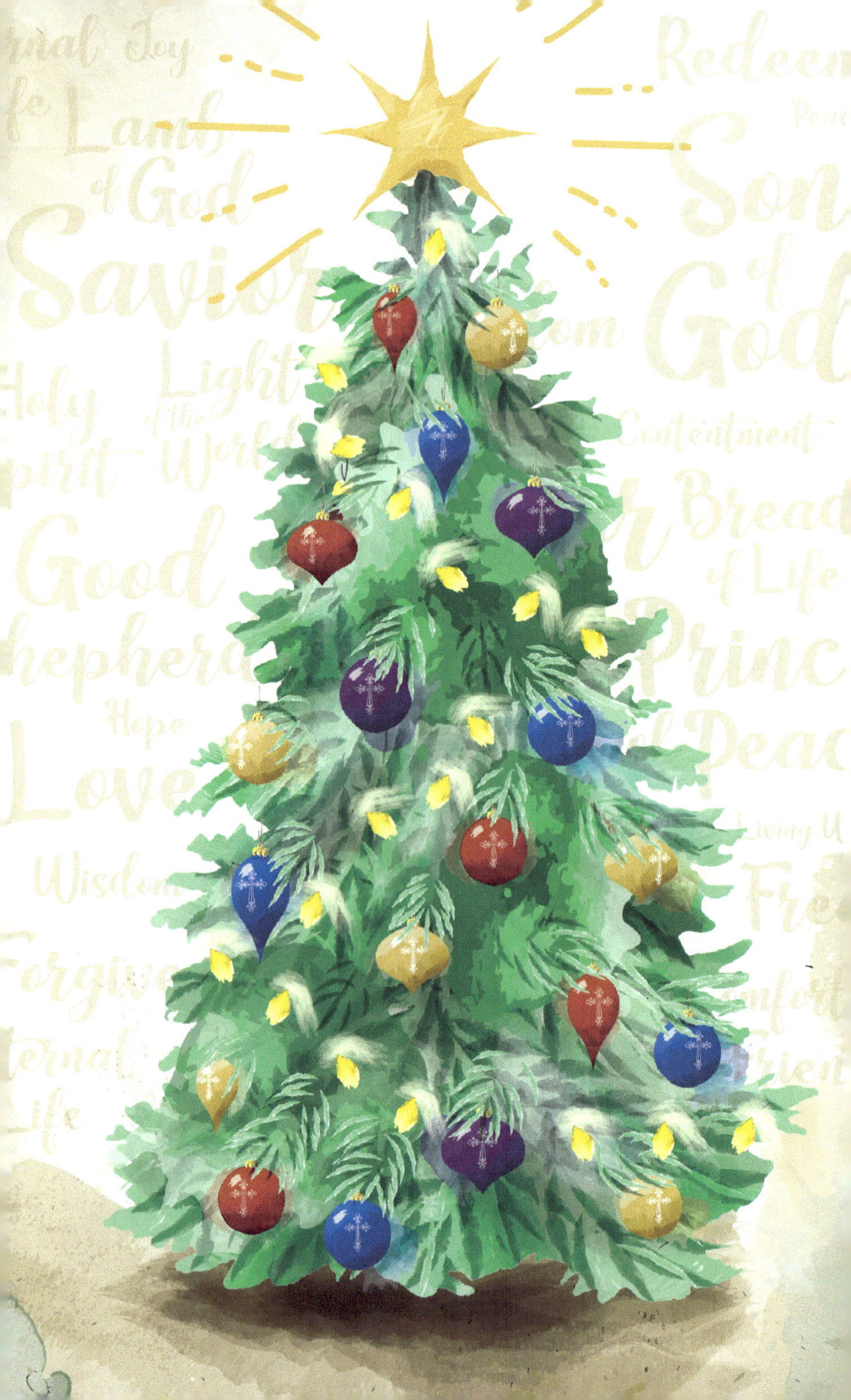

Joy
of God
Holy
Light
Contentment
Good
Hope
of Life

DAY 25
Merry Christmas

On this day, Celebrate Who Jesus Is and Why He Came

Isaiah 9:6
For a child will be born to us, a Son will be given to us; and the government will rest on His shoulders; and His name will be called Wonderful Counselor, mighty God, Eternal Father, Prince of Peace.

Matthew 1:21-23
And she will bear a Son, and you will call His name Jesus... for it is He who will save His people from their sins. Now all this took place that what was spoken by the Lord through the prophet might be fulfilled saying, "Behold, the virgin shall be with child, and shall bear a Son, and they shall call His name Immanuel, which translated means "God with us."

My Child,
Accept Me. Accept My gifts.

Jesus

For more of Chris Baxter's writing,
check out her website at
http://www.respitefortheweary.com

CPSIA information can be obtained
at www.ICGtesting.com
Printed in the USA
LVHW071107260922
729247LV00001B/1